Orchi

Nance Binks

This book is dedicated to family and friends without whose patience, support and understanding it would never have been published.

N.B.

Start to Finish Publishing
5 Whitecross Square
Cheltenham
GL53 7AY
UK
www.starttofinishpublishing.com

First published 2006

ISBN (2006) 0 9552641 0 3
(2007) 978 0 9552641 0 8

All photographs © Nance Binks except p.6 **a**, Liv Huey, and **h**, Dr Will Huey
Concept, editing and production by Myra Murby, Start to Finish
Design by Paul Manning

Printed and bound in Malta by Gutenberg Press

Contents

Foreword

Nance Binks came to Barbados in 1971, when her husband was appointed Professor of Chemistry at the University of the West Indies. She taught at St Ursula's School and Harrison College before becoming Headmistress of St Winifred's School in 1982. During her time at St Winifred's she wrote several books.

Nance has always loved orchids, and is a life member of the Barbados Orchid Society. She invested in Flower Forest, the parent company of Orchid World, and subsequently became a director of the company. Nance helped in the development of the Orchid World and then took on the task of looking after the orchid collection and training the staff. She also travelled to other West Indian islands and imported some interesting new orchids.

When we opened Orchid World, it was agreed that a book should be produced, but nobody got around to it until Nance took up the challenge. This book accurately illustrates the collection, can be recommended to all orchid lovers and will be a welcome addition to any garden library.

Richard Coghlan
March 2006

The Story of Orchid World

From Dream to Reality

Early in 1997 Orchid World was just a dream. Flower Forest, our beautifully landscaped woodland, was very successful, but we decided that the orchids deserved a special place of their own. We imagined a tranquil spot with flowing water and beautiful blooms. But where were we going to find it?

The search began, bearing in mind that we needed plenty of water, preferably rain, and considerate neighbours who wouldn't use chemical sprays which might drift and harm the orchids. Finally we found the ideal spot next door to The Caribbean Cane Breeding Station in a high rainfall area. Perfect! The bankrupt chicken farm dotted with rubbish and with a terrible smell may not have looked much at first glance, but it also had small limestone cliffs and gulleys on different levels which offered exciting landscaping possibilities. And the site was easy for visitors to get to.

a

b

c

a The new entrance **b** The beginning: uprooting and clearing was quite a task. **c** What is Richard thinking as he looks at the mess? **d** Starting to make orchid houses out of pigpens **e** The netting is now on the roof. Chairman Don in supervisory mode **f** We're getting there! **g** The pigpens are now taking shape as orchid houses **h** Not the most inspiring view **i** Late evening and still working

d

e

f

g

h

i

It took almost a year of hard work to create a delightful haven of beautiful orchids in a tranquil setting. And there were days when we wondered if we had bitten off more than we could chew. With Don Hill, the then company chairman as overseer and Richard Coghlan, well-known landscape artist providing the creative genius, the transformation gradually took place.

Nothing was wasted! Every rock was used, while the malodorous chicken manure provided instant nourishment to the newly planted Heliconia and Bougainvillea. The two derelict chicken houses were transformed into homes for numerous trays of Dendrobiums. The old pigpens on the lower level, just a series of stone pillars and a concrete channel, provided a basic structure for the Vandaceous orchids with a stream running through.

As roofing, to protect the orchids from the strong sun, we decided to use 40% shade-netting with 70% netting on a section of the 'nursery' while the 'walls' of these houses were simply 20% netting. The building which had been a garage with a solid roof became the 'show house' for Phalænopsis, Cattleyas and other more exotic orchids which required still more shade.

a

Meanwhile small 'bobcats' were used to move rocks and debris. Trees and hedges were planted to create specific areas. The old chicken-processing plant was gutted and rebuilt to become the entrance to the garden, the gift shop, restaurant and facilities. As water is so important, a 30,000-gallon water tank was constructed under the deck of the building. This tank captures as much rainwater as possible and is used to water the orchids as well as supplying the waterfall, the stream in the Vanda houses and the three fountains. The system has been designed so that the water is recycled.

a Lush vegetation due to chicken manure
b Outdoor vandas in place but roofing not yet finished on Vanda House **c** Bobcat at work

As opening day grew nearer the weather was definitely against us as torrential rain stopped us paving the car park which looked like a swimming pool! But it all worked out in the end and Orchid World was duly opened as planned on December 5th 1998 by the Prime Minister, the Honourable Owen Arthur. It has remained open ever since, from 9 a.m. to 5 p.m. daily.

The Team

The Head Gardener, T-Bert, along with Nicole, Deborah, Ryan and Orlando are loyal members of garden staff who helped with the creation of Orchid World from the outset. Others may come and go, but these five, with their incomparable knowledge, are essential to the smooth running of Orchid World. They look after the watering and feeding of all plants, as well as other chores such as sweeping, weeding and cutting hedges, trees and grass. A lot of work goes on behind the scenes and every morning the orchids are inspected. In the Show houses those in bloom are placed in prominent positions while those which have finished flowering may be moved back to the nursery. The staff are invariably pleasant and more than happy to answer visitors' questions. They even help push the occasional wheelchair up that final slope.

a

b

a Cutting the ribbon
b The Prime Minister on opening day. Fortunately it wasn't raining.

c

d

c Deborah by a bed of Antigua Heath
d Nicole watering/misting the plants in
the nursery e Ryan, planting or weeding?
f Orlando and Nicole hanging baskets in the
Gazebo prior to a wedding g T-Bert, Head
Gardener, showing off the Dendrobiums

e

f

g

Sourcing the Orchids

As we needed to have orchids in flower when we opened, we had to order them before the houses were ready. This meant constructing temporary homes for them such as trays on which to put the Dendrobiums (after potting) and hanging wire frames from the roof of the same Dendrobium house as a temporary home for the Vandas, etc.

a *The newly arrived orchids need a home – all in the only house with a roof!* **b** *One of the donated Calanthes* **c** *The orchids are shipped in these boxes. Progress: poles and wire!*

W e asked for advice and help from local experts, and we are very grateful for that. They gave freely of their knowledge of growing and breeding orchids and even contributed many plants. We have gained so much knowledge from them and do appreciate the time they have given in helping get the project up and running. The ground orchids, Spathoglottis, were all bought locally, and the Calanthes, which flower once a year, were a gift from a local enthusiast.

But we needed large quantities and so we decided to order a large consignment from Thailand the previous April. That way the orchids would be at their peak for the opening in December. Now we bring orchids from Singapore, Hawaii, Miami and nearby Trinidad, but initially Thailand appeared to have exactly what we needed quickly and in the right quantities. We wanted free-flowering (several times per year) indoor and outdoor plants such as Vandaceous orchids and Dendrobiums together with a smaller consignment of Cattleyas and Phalænopsis. The most important criteria was similarity of climate. For example, we own two Cymbidiums, normally very successful in temperate climates, but they are not very happy plants in Orchid World.

c

In Barbados many orchids are at their best from late February to April. Fortunately for us this does not apply to every orchid! For instance, one real star, the Grammatophyllum, usually blooms later than April. We have three specific varieties, each of which flowers at a different time.

Our most spectacular one, Grammatophyllum Speciosum, flowered in August/September. This plant was given to us six years ago and had never flowered before. When it did it was well worth the wait! Flowering out-of-doors in a fairly large pot, it must be about eight feet in height and at least six feet across. There were twelve spikes and each one had approximately one hundred and fifty blooms. I could only count one set as I couldn't reach the rest! At the base of each spike were one or two blooms of a shape uncharacteristic of the orchid.

The majority of orchid flowers have bilateral symmetry – i.e. one axis of symmetry – five distinct petals and a protruding lip. The blooms at the base of this fascinating plant had four petals and a very small elongated lip. Were these malformed or just a peculiarity of this particular plant?

a Grammatophylum Speciosum: twelve spikes with approximately 150 blooms on each! **b** Grammatophylum Speciosum: a close-up view **c** The flowers at the base of each stem are a completely different form. **d** An interesting variation in shape! **e** Nicole stands beside the plant to give some idea of its height. **f** Visitors admire the Grammatophylum Speciosum.

c

d

e

f

The Tour

Visiting the Garden

People visit Orchid World throughout the year and so we make sure that there is always something to see. You can take the short route or the long route, shown on the plan, and spend anything from forty-five minutes to the whole day if you want to.

The best time of day is early or late when the blooms are most fragrant. Even when it is raining the garden has great charm and the scents are enhanced. We provide umbrellas, and showers rarely last long.

Don't forget your camera! It is pure delight to the photographer. Just make sure that you have enough film or a fully charged battery if you prefer digital.

a Richard (in red T-shirt) with a group of four guides
b Gordon and Ena Baxter of Baxters' Foods: old friends who love Orchid World. This was their 20th visit to Barbados **c** Choose your pathway.

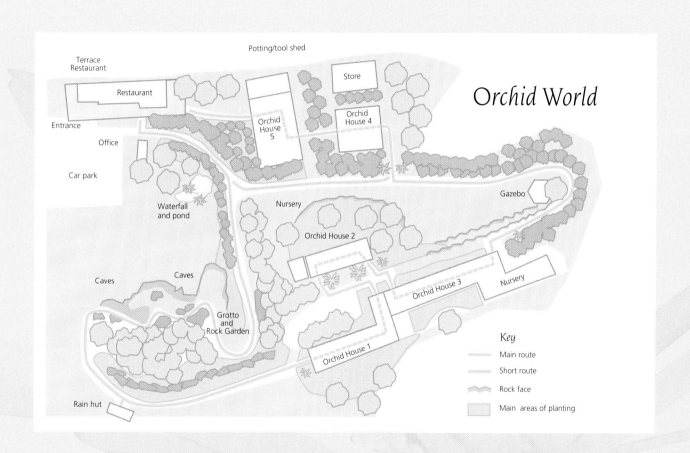

Potting/tool shed

Terrace
Restaurant

Store

Restaurant

Orchid
House
5

Orchid
House 4

Orchid World

Entrance

Office

Car park

Nursery

Waterfall
and pond

Gazebo

Orchid House 2

Caves

Caves

Orchid House 3

Nursery

Grotto
and
Rock Garden

Orchid House 1

Key

Main route

Short route

Rock face

Main areas of planting

Rain hut

Setting off

From the car park, enter the building by the entrance on your left, to the ticket booth. Pass through the gift shop and the entrance to the garden is via the steps just beyond the restaurant, on your right. Toilet facilities are on the left. A separate entrance via a ramp is provided for wheelchair visitors before you reach the restaurant.

Immediately ahead of you is the office – built to resemble a Bajan chattel-house. You may be fortunate enough to see a family of monkeys playing among the trees behind.

a

b

a *The new entrance to the ticket booth* **b** *The steps where the tour starts* **c** *Previously the start of the tour, this path is now used only by wheelchairs.* **d** *The first group of outdoor orchids at the left of the office* **e** *Can you see the monkey? It can usually be seen behind the office or running across the carpark.*

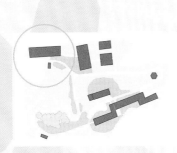

Here to the left of the office is the first arrangement of orchids. All the orchids on the specially designed frames (Vandaceous), would normally grow perhaps two hundred feet above the leaf-canopy in the rainforest. We have just arranged them at eye-level for your enjoyment but we do try to give them the conditions in which they thrive best. Underneath the decorative gravel are sheets of matting which prevent too many of the roots from growing into the soil. Wherever you see this gravel, whether indoor or out, there will be matting underneath. These plants are epiphytes or air-plants – they only use the trees for support in nature. If they have too much contact with the ground, especially as young plants, they tend to become waterlogged and susceptible to disease. About 75% of the world's orchids belong to this group, the rest being terrestrials.

a

I n the foreground are ground orchids (Spathoglottis), which require totally different conditions. The soil must be fairly friable, so not heavy but crumbly. We achieve this by mixing large quantities of horse manure and bagasse, a waste sugar product, with the soil.

a *Vandaceous orchids near the office. Note the netting.* **b** *Ground orchid in bloom*

b

Follow the pathway between banks of Antigua Heath, left, also known as Firecracker or Coral plant and Tabernæmontana, the Star Jasmine on the right. On the left is the decorative plaque identifying the tree planted by The Prime Minister when he declared the Orchid World open. This tree is Harpullia Zanguebarica, commonly known as Black Pearl.

Planted by
The Right Hon. Owen Arthur M.P.
Prime Minister
on
5th December 1998

b

a

The pathway now divides into the **short walk** or **main trail**. Both are shown on the map. The short walk leads directly to the Gazebo past arrangements of orchids, then back through the Dendrobium houses. Some of our visitors find the last upward slope a little distressing, so this alternative route was devised for them.

a Tabernæmontana (Star jasmine) just before the waterfall **b** Plaque by tree planted by the Prime Minister on opening day (Black Pearl) **c** The view along the 'short walk,' from the sign.

c

Trees and Trickling Water

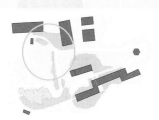

Behind the hedging of bamboo grass is a cleverly contrived waterfall. You can hear the pleasant sound of running water which trickles down the rock face to two small ponds at the base (right). The orchids in front of the palms (left) are Aranda Noorah Alsagoff. These generally flower profusely but may require more light than is available in this area. The fascinating root structure of the Ficus (Bearded fig-tree) and the Mahogany trees give an excellent backdrop.

The banks of Pittosporum and Leah are no more than seven years old and require constant pruning otherwise the orchids (right) do not flower as often as we would like, as it can be far too shady. The main purpose of these hedges is to provide an element of privacy from other groups on the lower level. On the right are groups of Vandas, Mokaras and Arandas, then a bed of Spathoglottis. As you round the corner you see a line of Vanda Miss Agnes Joaquim, the National flower of Singapore.

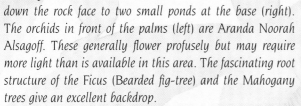

a

b

a T-Bert has just turned on the waterfall pump – all contrived. **b** Left of first slope, incredible root structure on Ficus **c** The descending path to the Grotto **d** Left of path, Pittaspruce and Leah hedging **e** Left, Aranda Miss Agnes Joaquim, the national flower of Singapore. On way to Grotto.

c

d

e

The Grotto

There is now a distinct drop in temperature as you enter the Grotto. The groundcover 'Creeping Charlie' has taken over and covers the rock face. The natural caves, which we have not yet fully explored, contain ferns and who knows what else. The Traveller's Palm has at last developed some sense of direction and the miniature Bamboo is flourishing on the slope. The palm is said to provide direction and water to the weary traveller in its natural habitat of the desert.

Initially we put orchids on the trees but they never really flourished; possibly it is too shady, but it also was due to monkey interference. In the early morning this is their playground. Here we have placed the first of the numerous benches scattered throughout the garden.

a

a Grotto – note orchids attached to trees
b Cave in Grotto **c** Grotto

b

c

Ginger Lilies, Orchids and the Fishtail Palm

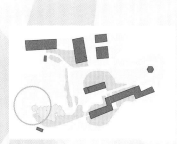

The path rises gently past red Ginger Lilies on the left and groups of Vandaceous orchids on both sides. The view across the cane fields is quite spectacular especially when the caneflower is in bloom. In November and December this looks like a vast expanse of white feather dusters. Should it rain, head for the rain hut (right), the only covered area until you reach the Show House.

The path now veers left towards the first house of 'indoor' plants. Behind the Antiguan Heath (left) is an extensive group of Duranta Repens, the Golden Dewdrop. This bush is very attractive when covered in yellow berries and pale blue flowers.

a First visitors after opening. Just look at those cane arrows! **b** View of canefields from path – near rainhut **c** Rainhut **d** Path to Ascocenda House with Aranda Noorah Alsagoff **e** Blue Aranda Noorah Alsagoff

a

b

c

d

e

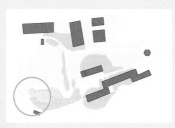

On the right a large Mahogany and an Almond tree provide support for Schomburgkia and Oncidiums. These are attached by nails or by tying the plant with wire to the host tree. The beds of Euphorbiaceæ are rather fascinating and were grown by Dr Graham, also a director of Orchid World. The Fishtail Palm, better known as the Rasta palm because of its hairstyle, and the yet-to-flower Grammatophyllum on the right are interesting features.

a

b

c

d

a *Wives of Commonwealth finance ministers during tour*
b *Duranta Repens on left of path* **c** *Path approach to Ascocenda House* **d** *The distinctive Fishtail Palm*

The Asocenda House

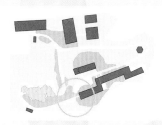

W e now enter the Ascocenda House. You can choose your path as both lead to the same exit. The majority of these orchids are Ascocendas or Vanda crossed with Ascocenda. Under natural conditions these would grow beneath the leaf canopy, perhaps one hundred and eighty feet up, well above eye-level. They have no contact with the ground so we have tried to give them the conditions they prefer, watering by hosepipe at least twice per day when there is no rainfall. The same hosepipe with a 'proportioner' bottle attached is used to feed the orchids once a week with the correct dose of liquid feed. Under very hot, dry conditions, the pathway may be soaked around midday to give extra humidity to the atmosphere.

a

a The Ascocenda House as it was in the early days. It no longer has trays of Dendrobiums
b The Ascocenda House: left path **c** The Ascocenda House: right path **d** The Ascocenda House: both paths

b

c

d

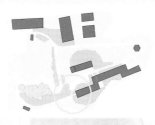

The stream, now lined with moss-covered coral stones also adds to the humidity, as does the variegated ground cover under some sections. We try to keep the planting on the outside at a reasonable height, allowing a good breeze to blow through the houses. This helps reduce pest infection and encourages healthier growth. As you near the exit notice some of the miniature orchids such as Rhyncocentrum, Rhyncovanda, Ascocentrum etc.

We are always delighted when a keiki develops on a mature plant. I understand that keiki means 'baby' in Hawaian, so baby remains attached to 'mother' and as it grows we than have a larger plant, hopefully with spikes on both.

a

a *Miniatures near the exit (left) of the Ascocenda House* **b** *Not quite so 'mini,' but lots of blooms* **c** *Another stunning example*

b

c

The orchids are not all labelled as it is a time-consuming exercise, but we have attempted to identify as many as possible. Do look out for the 'SCENTED' labels. A particularly strong perfume comes from Vanda Kampiranon x Ascocenda Seechang.

Immediately ahead of you as you exit is the Grammatophyllum Speciosum previously mentioned. Now that it has bloomed once in August and September 2005 we wonder if this will be an annual event. Only time will tell!

a Vanda Kampiranon x Ascocenda Seechang (Scented)
b Ascocenda Laksi "I Q-Glade' **c** Ascocenda Anant Gold **d** Ascocenda John de Bias (pink) **e** Ascocenda Thepthong **f** Ascocenda Princess Mikasa **g** Ascocenda Surat Spot

c

d

e

f

g

The Show House

a

Across the courtyard and past the potted Epidendrums on the left, we reach the Show House. A small boy approaching this entrance said he could smell a vanilla chocolate milk shake! I would not be so specific but understand his thinking. The scent comes from a large arrangement of Oncidium Sharry Baby. These seem to flower for several months, or it may be that we are fortunate enough to have a large quantity of plants which bloom successively rather than simultaneously.

Although orchids are generally fairly robust, we do ask visitors not to touch the flowers. When the petals are bruised by too much 'feeling' this results in another 'dead-head' consigned to the garbage!

a *and* **b** *Oncidium Sharry Baby*

b

The pots of Asparagus Sprengeri around the orchid trays (used extensively in the Dendrobium houses) were there for a very practical reason in the early days. The edges of the trays were somewhat unsightly as well as dangerous to clothing – bare wire spikes! The Asparagus fern was so useful in concealing this. A visitor was highly intrigued by what she thought was our watering system – hosepipe running round the edges of the trays! All our watering is done manually via the old-fashioned system of hosepipe. What she observed was old hosepipe cut longitudinally and tied on to bare wire edges to reduce damage to clothing from the sharp edges!

a Cattleya Percivaliana **b** Oncidium Sweet Sugar **c** Brassocattleya Maikai `Mayumi' **d** Phalænopsis Valentine – a tiny flower! Just compare with the small pot behind.

b

a

c

d

The majority of plants here have different requirements from the Vandas, Dendrobiums etc. These must not be over-watered and do not like direct sun and so the roof is partially tin, partially Perspex. Since so many of these orchids such as Cattleya, Phalænopsis, Brassia, Brassocattleya and Brassolæliocattleya flower annually or biannually that we do replace them frequently. A flower in bloom may last up to two months but when the flower is over the plant is replaced and sent to rest in the nursery until another spike appears.

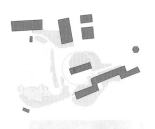

a Phalænopsis Giat Gong
b Brassidium Fly Away 'Miumi'
c In Show House: Brassavola Nodosa **d** A particularly beautiful Brassolæliocattleya (BLC)
e Brassolæliocattleya Greenwich 'Elmhurst' **f** So beautiful – and scented! **g** Brassolæliocattleya Golden Tang

b

a

c

d

e

f

g

h

Before you leave this house do admire the Butterfly orchid 'Papilio' on display by the door. This beauty was acquired in Trinidad and has bloomed, one butterfly at a time, almost incessantly since its first flowering. There are a few other orchids from Trinidad on display, when in flower of course! The Stanhopea Grandiflora has a superb perfume when first open but smells dreadful once the bloom begins to fade. This plant is best grown in a basket, thus allowing the pendulous inflorescences to grow through the sides and bottom of the container. Another with similar habit is the Gongora Maculata, not the most attractive but different. The spike hanging over the side of the container has a profusion of flowers, likened to 'birds in flight.' Unfortunately both the Stanhopea and the Gongora flower for a short time compared with the majority of our orchids.

a

b

a *and* **b** *The Butterfly Orchid, Oncidium Papilio, from Trinidad* **c** *From Rinidad: Gongora. Not so attractive but interesting nonetheless* **d** *Stanhope*

46

Many of these are seasonal. You may see a spectacular display of Oncidiums, or Calanthes. The Cattleyas may be in full bloom or even the Phalænopsis. It really does depend so much on the time of year and weather conditions. Over-watering or over-feeding can be as harmful as too little. Quite a number of these orchids are scented – just look out for the labels!

We hope to develop the area behind this house in the very near future. At present it is home to many hanging baskets which, when in flower, are 'promoted' to the Show House.

c

d

The Vanda House

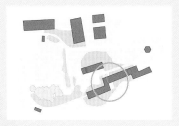

Once again we cross the courtyard to the Vanda House, passing through arrangements of outdoor orchids. The majority of these were the first plants tied to the frames before Orchid World was officially opened. They have continued to bloom profusely ever since.

Notice the Grammatophyllum Elegans attached to the fencing and to the sides of the Vanda House. These usually flower with long cascading spikes in July and August.

a Between the Show house and Vanda House past pots of Epidendrums **b** Note the roots of this Grammatophyllum Elegans – a rather different structure **c** Visitors admiring the Vandas **d** Vanda Praneet x Tessellata

a

b

c

d

Quite a number of the Vandas have a fragrance, not always the most pleasing but fragrant nevertheless. The blooms vary tremendously in size, colour and even texture. A group which I find particularly interesting is the *Vanda Gold Spot x Vanda Insignis*. These hang on the left near the exit. They are all the same Vanda cross, almost identical in markings, but have tremendous variation in colour.

The stream is a continuation of that in the previous house and is home to fish and numerous frogs. A young visitor reckoned that she counted eighty-three! The pond and fountain are serviced by the same pump. On the right is the original nursery, variously called hospital, nursery or mortuary, depending on the state of the plant consigned to this area!

a

b

c

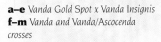

d

e

a–e *Vanda Gold Spot x Vanda Insignis*
f–m *Vanda and Vanda/Ascocenda crosses*

f

g

h

i

j

k

l

m

Fossils and the Bearded Fig

Before you start the slow climb to the Gazebo, do look at the coralstone fossils on the rock face. An eminent geologist said that these indicated that two million years ago, Barbados was totally underwater. The roots of the Ficus, or Bearded Fig/Banyan Tree are quite spectacular. With heavy rain these roots swell to such an extent that we have had several falls of rock – fortunately not on the orchids.

Visitors find the leaves of the Cecropia tree quite unusual. Locally these are widely used in floral decoration. Throughout the Caribbean this tree is believed to have various medicinal properties administered as a 'bush tea.' It is also said to be an aphrodisiac!

The Bougainvillea hedge on the right hides the somewhat functional building of the Cane Breeding Station. When the cane is high, this is not an issue but by June this is cut and the view is a rather ugly building behind a field of stubble.

a

a *Coralstone fossils on rock face, left as you exit the Vanda House* **b** *Ficus above the cliff: roots can be seen opposite the Vanda House growing through the rock face* **c** *The tree behind is the Cecropia*

b

c

The Gazebo

The Gazebo is multifunctional. A pleasant resting place after the climb up the slope, it is frequently the venue for weddings. The centre pole is adorned with orchid plants and baskets filled with orchids are hung around the edge of the overhangs. A marquee on the lawn with seating provides space for guests. The reception is usually held in the restaurant area. The view across the valley is quite spectacular, from Andrews Sugar Factory on the far right to the parish of St Thomas on the left. This area was once known as Sweet Bottom, but is now renamed Sweet Vale. I am sure you can imagine how spectacular it really is when the cane arrows are in full bloom!

As you stand on the lawn here, visualise the caves beneath! Apparently it is possible to walk upright around a massive rock in the middle. If you really wish to investigate – at your own risk, of course – the entrance is on the slope immediately ahead of you beyond the line of orchids.

a

a The Gazebo **b** Arranging orchids on central pole in the Gazebo prior to a wedding party **c** View across the valley from the Gazebo

b

c

Heliconia, Bougainvillea and Dendrobium

Once the rainy season is over the Bougainvillea comes into full bloom in a variety of colours. As we turn right towards the first house of Dendrobiums, do stop to admire the large group of Heliconia. This is where the bulk of the rather odorous chicken manure was buried.

a

b

a *Ground orchids in bed behind exit sign* **b** *On left before entering first Dendrobium House* **c** *The fountain in the Dendrobium House is actually working!* **d** *General view in the first Dendrobium House* **e** *A grand display of Dendrobium Thongchai Gold* **f** *The Dendrobium House*

As we enter this next house we notice a slight drop in temperature, largely due to the pond and fountain, using recycled water of course, adding moisture to the atmosphere. All the orchids in this section require pots. The mixture is part broken 'crock', part aliflor, with a few pieces of charcoal (definitely not the barbecue type) which is added to help 'sweeten' the mix. Dendrobiums dislike being waterlogged and this seems to be their preferred medium. We used to use tree bark in the mix, but this degenerated too quickly into a mud-like concoction which encouraged the growth of weeds and was an ideal breeding ground for pests.

Nor do Dendrobiums thrive when housed in too large a pot. They are perfectly happy with roots extending outside the pot. Our only difficulty is that the plant often becomes top-heavy and falls over. Then we just place the existing pot inside a slightly larger one.

c

d

e

f

The life of a Dendrobium appears to be about four years so the majority of the original ones have been replaced. The suppliers are constantly producing new varieties though some of the old favourites are still the best, Emma White, Thongchai Gold, Jacquelyn Thomas, to name a few.

c

a

b

d

e

f

h

i

g

i

l

a–h A superb collection of Dendrobiums
i Dendrobium Tubrim Velvet x Dendrobium Classic
Gams. **j** Dendrobium Caral Goo **k** Dendrobium
Meesangil **l** Dendrobium Rinabha – Jaq. Concert.

k

The Pond House

Arrangements of Vanda Miss Agnes Joaquim with Tabernæmontana in the background line the pathway to the next house. By the entrance you will see the vine, Hoya. When in flower this exudes a powerful perfume which very few of the Dendrobiums do. Once again this is largely a home for Dendrobiums except for the hanging Ascocendas round the pond. Near the exit there is frequently an interesting variety of whatever gives that extra touch of colour. This may be Cattleya Skinneri or Grammatophyllum Elegans, depending largely on time of year. The choice of arrangement is frequently governed by what can be easily moved from its original setting. A Jewel Orchid hides rather insignificantly among the foliage on the right of the exit. Its leaf is very attractive even if the flower is unremarkable. Several large Bird's Nest as well as Maidenhair ferns add to the ambience.

a

a Between Dendrobium Houses
b Dendrobiums **c** The Dendrobium House as it is now **d** Dendrobiums displayed on the 'walls' **e** Right of exit: Jewel orchid (Ludisia Discolor), partially hidden by the orchid

b

The covered area on the right is the main 'workshop'. Here much of the potting is done, and baskets are prepared for the gazebo weddings. All the supplies for the orchids are stored here. This area is a hive of activity when a new shipment of plants arrives. We try to get them out of the boxes in which they are shipped as soon as possible. This helps minimise deterioration.

d

c

e

A slight incline through luscious vegetation, Ixora, Antiguan Heath among others takes you to the end of your tour. You are invited to browse in the gift shop, enjoy a cool drink in the restaurant and even buy an orchid from our newly installed plant-house to the right.

We do hope you have enjoyed the tour, whether in person or via this book.

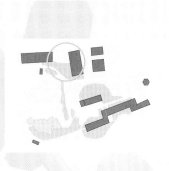

a

b

a Path up to the restaurant. Tour over!
b Round the last bend *c Building set up for a wedding* *d Baskets with orchid arrangements for a wedding*

c

d

More About Orchids

Caring for Orchids

We are frequently asked how to care for an orchid, so that it looks as healthy as most of ours seem to do. The answer is not as simple as one might think. But there are a large number of publications dealing with the subject. My first question is generally 'which country, what type of climate'? There is no one answer. I would recommend that you ask your supplier for basic guidelines on watering, feeding and general care. Once the leaves look green and healthy and the plant is in bloom, then you will soon find out if you are administering the correct TLC. The plant will remain looking healthy if all is well and continue to bloom for several weeks. Insufficient light usually results in a reasonably healthy-looking green plant but no spikes. So move it into more light until you find the best location.

Like any other plant, orchids require constant care, though most of them are not as fragile as is generally believed. Water is an absolute essential. Here at Orchid World we are fortunate that we have a constant supply of rainwater for most of the year, thanks to Richard's foresight in building the storage tank at the outset. Unless it has rained overnight the first task every morning is watering, first outdoor, then in. The afternoon process is reversed, no earlier than 3.30 p.m. Apart from the ferns, the plants in the lower Show House require watering two or three times per week, but this too may vary and has to be carefully monitored – not too much, not too little. During the rainy season the Dendrobiums rarely need to be watered but not so in the dry period. Again, careful monitoring is essential. The wet and dry seasons vary somewhat from year to year, but mid-Dececember to April/May (tourist season) is generally the drier time.

Some orchids require no water during 'rest' periods. The Calanthe is a typical example, as is the Dendrobium Superbum. When in full flower, in April/May, this has to be the most highly scented of all our orchids.

'Dead-heading' is another daily 'must'. If this chore is neglected the plants soon begin to look neglected.

Almost every orchid-grower seems to have his or her own theories about the best treatment. Ask three enthusiasts for advice and you are liable to get three different answers! Trial and error or learn by your mistakes is often the answer, though this can be costly. We can only say what has been reasonably successful in our situation. Barbados may be a small island but conditions do vary. What works in the north may not work in the south. Near the sea or inland, there are so many variables. Some areas have considerably less rainfall than others, some less breeze. Different orchids seem to flourish in different parts of the island. For instance, we have not had great success with Phalænopsis, but will persevere since this comprises such a large group of so many attractive blooms.

Orchid groups

We have over 30,000 orchids but they fall into several basic groups, with numerous variations within each group.

The large majority are epiphytes requiring no contact with soil, and are grown in pots, baskets (wood, wire or Guatemalan tree-fern) or on pieces of wood (Cordia is a favourite), chunks of tree-fern, bark or on seasoned driftwood. Some of these are attached to tree-trunks, Schomburgkia and Oncidium. Our outdoor Vandas, Mokara, Aranda, etc., only require support. Hence the attractively devised wire frames. Indoors, the Ascocendas and other Vandaceous that need some shade just hang freely, attached to a wire for support. The Cattleyas, Phalænopsis, Brassavola etc, are in pots.

The terrestrials are the ground orchids, Spatthoglottis, mentioned previously, all bought from a local source. The Epidendrums are grown out of doors in fairly large pots.

We occasionally make use of dried coconut husks as these do help retain moisture. However, if too wet they rot very quickly and so may the orchid roots.

Orchid growing in Barbados

All containers and material such as broken crock must be clean. Sterilise if this is recycled material.

Cattleya: Place in clay or plastic pot in very porous media, broken crock and charcoal (horticultural), fir bark or tree fern, a little perlite. For good flowering, bright light is essential. Leaves should be a medium green colour. Plenty of water is required during the growing period but less when resting.

Dendrobiums: Pot in clay or plastic, small rather than large; a length of wire tied to the bottom will help ensure that the plant stays firmly in the pot. Broken crock, aliflor, a little charcoal is our preferred medium. Avoid overwatering. If the leaves are dark green but rarely flower, the plant requires more light.

Phalænopsis: Pot as for Cattleya. These prefer fairly heavy shade, watering two or three times per week, with light misting in between, but so much depends on the potting medium used. Constant inspection is essential.

Vandaceous orchids: Tie these on poles or wires. If the plant has little root structure, place the healthiest root in a small vial filled with water. This provides constant water to the plant but should be watched carefully for development of algæ. We cover new outdoor Vandas with netting in the early stages to prevent over exposure to strong sunlight. Wet the plants twice per day if rain does not do this for you!

Know your Vanda. Should it be in full sun or part shade? The Mokara, broad-leafed, will grow in full sun but the strap-leaf Vanda prefers part shade. Though many orchids like light and sun, few do too well in the hot midday sun in Barbados.

Feeding and fertilising

Weakly, weekly is the best maxim! There are so many products available from suppliers — just read the instructions very carefully. Orchids need nitrogen, phosphorous and potassium for healthy growth. This is quoted on the container as a balanced fertiliser i.e. 20-20-20 or 10-10-10. For mature plants in normal potting material, this is generally the recommended mix. Blossom booster, 10-30-20, high in phosphorous, is used occasionally to encourage blooming and healthy growth. Use half a teaspoon per gallon of water per week for mature plants and a somewhat weaker mixture for seedlings.

Once per month we give Orchid World plants, lawns, etc., a treatment of Epsom salts, one teaspoon to a gallon of water. A tour guide was overheard to say that we gave everything a laxative each month! In fact the Epsom salts enhances the greenness and makes for healthier plants. Try it on your roses!

P.S. Have you read The Orchid Thief?

The Plates

Rhyncostylis Alliance

Spathoglottis
terrestrial or ground orchid

Aranda Noorah Alsagoff

Miniatures: Rhynocovanda

Vanda Kampiranon
x Asocenda Seechang

Brassocattleya Maikai 'Mayumi'

Brassolæliocattleya Greenwich
'Elmhurst'

Vanda Gold Spot
x Vanda Insignis

Asocenda hybrid

Potinara Montaburi Fancy x
Lælocattleya Mari's Song

Dendrobium Meesangil

Dendrobium Rinabha –
Jaq. Concert